EVERY CLOUD HAS A SILVER LINING

summersdale

EVERY CLOUD HAS A SILVER LINING

An Hachette UK Company
www.hachette.co.uk

Summersdale Publishers Ltd
Part of Octopus Publishing Group Limited
Carmelite House
50 Victoria Embankment
LONDON
EC4Y 0DZ
UK

www.summersdale.com

Printed and bound in China

ISBN: 978-1-78783-540-5

Substantial discounts on bulk quantities of Summersdale books
are available to corporations, professional associations and other
organizations. For details contact general enquiries: telephone:
+44 (0) 1243 771107 or email: enquiries@summersdale.com.

To..

From....................................

Storms make oaks take deeper root.

GEORGE HERBERT

IF YOU'RE GOING
TO WALK ON THIN
ICE, YOU MIGHT AS
WELL DANCE.

KARIN GILLESPIE

Start each day with a positive thought

EVEN IF YOU FALL
ON YOUR FACE,
YOU'RE STILL
MOVING FORWARD.

ROBERT C. GALLAGHER

"

I'M NOT AFRAID OF STORMS,
FOR I'M LEARNING
HOW TO SAIL MY SHIP.

LOUISA MAY ALCOTT

"

HAPPINESS IS NOT
AN IDEAL OF REASON,
BUT OF IMAGINATION.

IMMANUEL KANT

Rain is
just confetti
from the sky

The optimist sees the doughnut,
but the pessimist sees the hole.

McLANDBURGH WILSON

FAILURE IS ANOTHER STEPPING
STONE TO GREATNESS.

OPRAH WINFREY

Positive mind,
positive vibes,
positive life

WHETHER YOU
THINK YOU CAN
OR YOU THINK
YOU CAN'T,
YOU'RE RIGHT.

HENRY FORD

PERHAPS OUR EYES NEED TO BE WASHED BY OUR TEARS ONCE IN A WHILE, SO THAT WE CAN SEE LIFE WITH A CLEARER VIEW AGAIN.

ALEX TAN

Success is due
less to ability
than to zeal.

CHARLES BUXTON

I AM AN OPTIMIST.
IT DOES NOT
SEEM TOO MUCH
USE BEING
ANYTHING ELSE.

WINSTON CHURCHILL

IF WE HAD NO WINTER,
THE SPRING WOULD NOT
BE SO PLEASANT: IF WE
DID NOT SOMETIMES
TASTE OF ADVERSITY,
PROSPERITY WOULD
NOT BE SO WELCOME.

ANNE BRADSTREET

Say yes
to new
adventures

There is always
a bright side

66

ANGELS CAN FLY BECAUSE
THEY TAKE THEMSELVES LIGHTLY.

G. K. CHESTERTON

99

WHEN ASKED IF MY
CUP IS HALF-FULL
OR HALF-EMPTY, MY
ONLY RESPONSE IS
THAT I AM THANKFUL
I HAVE A CUP.

ANONYMOUS

The misfortunes hardest to bear
are those which never come.

AMY LOWELL

If it doesn't
challenge you,
it doesn't
change you

WHENEVER YOU FALL,
PICK SOMETHING UP.

OSWALD AVERY

A POSITIVE ATTITUDE MAY NOT SOLVE ALL YOUR PROBLEMS, BUT IT WILL ANNOY ENOUGH PEOPLE TO MAKE IT WORTH THE EFFORT.

HERM ALBRIGHT

*Stay
sunny on
the inside*

YOUR HARDEST
TIMES OFTEN LEAD
TO THE GREATEST
MOMENTS OF
YOUR LIFE.

ROY T. BENNETT

The darkest
hour has only
60 minutes.

MORRIS MANDEL

LIFE ISN'T HOW
YOU SURVIVE THE
THUNDERSTORM,
BUT HOW YOU DANCE
IN THE RAIN.

ADAM YOUNG

Happy is as
happy does

WHEREVER
YOU GO, NO
MATTER WHAT
THE WEATHER,
ALWAYS BRING
YOUR OWN
SUNSHINE.

ANTHONY J. D'ANGELO

IN THE LAND OF THE BLIND,
THE ONE-EYED MAN IS KING.

ERASMUS

It always seems
impossible until
it is done

POSITIVE ANYTHING
IS BETTER THAN
NEGATIVE NOTHING.

ELBERT HUBBARD

A kick in the teeth
may be the best thing
in the world for you.

WALT DISNEY

ALWAYS LAUGH WHEN YOU CAN.
IT IS CHEAP MEDICINE.

LORD BYRON

Splash
around
in life's
puddles

TOUGH TIMES NEVER LAST, BUT TOUGH PEOPLE DO!

ROBERT H. SCHULLER

I DON'T THINK
OF ALL THE
MISERY, BUT OF
THE BEAUTY THAT
STILL REMAINS.

ANNE FRANK

Dare to begin

Life is either a daring adventure or nothing.

HELEN KELLER

THE BEST WAY TO
SECURE FUTURE
HAPPINESS IS TO
BE AS HAPPY AS
IS RIGHTFULLY
POSSIBLE TODAY.

CHARLES W. ELIOT

HAPPINESS
CONSISTS NOT
IN HAVING
MUCH, BUT IN
BEING CONTENT
WITH LITTLE.

MARGUERITE GARDINER

Too many people
miss the silver lining
because they're
expecting gold

TO CLIMB STEEP HILLS REQUIRES SLOW PACE AT FIRST.

WILLIAM SHAKESPEARE

YOU CAN'T BE BRAVE
IF YOU'VE ONLY HAD
WONDERFUL THINGS
HAPPEN TO YOU.

MARY TYLER MOORE

Don't be
the same
– be better

Nothing is a waste of time
if you use the experience wisely.

AUGUSTE RODIN

THERE ARE ALWAYS FLOWERS FOR
THOSE WHO WANT TO SEE THEM.

HENRI MATISSE

BUT THE MAN WORTH WHILE IS THE ONE WHO WILL SMILE, WHEN EVERYTHING GOES DEAD WRONG.

ELLA WHEELER WILCOX

Keep hope
in your heart

AERODYNAMICALLY,
THE BUMBLEBEE
SHOULDN'T BE
ABLE TO FLY, BUT
THE BUMBLEBEE
DOESN'T KNOW IT
SO IT GOES ON
FLYING ANYWAY.

MARY KAY ASH

DREAMS ARE RENEWABLE.
NO MATTER WHAT OUR
AGE OR CONDITION, THERE
ARE STILL UNTAPPED
POSSIBILITIES WITHIN US.

DALE TURNER

Your life is
as good as
your mindset

Be happy.
It's one way
of being wise.

COLETTE

WE ARE ALL
IN THE GUTTER,
BUT SOME OF US
ARE LOOKING
AT THE STARS.

OSCAR WILDE

A MAN'S REACH SHOULD EXCEED HIS GRASP, OR WHAT'S A HEAVEN FOR?

ROBERT BROWNING

Old ways won't open new doors

THE GRAND ESSENTIALS
TO HAPPINESS IN THIS
LIFE ARE SOMETHING
TO DO, SOMETHING TO
LOVE, AND SOMETHING
TO HOPE FOR.

GEORGE WASHINGTON BURNAP

No problem can withstand
the assault of sustained thinking.

VOLTAIRE

Bad days help
you appreciate
the good ones

ONE MAY WALK OVER THE HIGHEST
MOUNTAIN ONE STEP AT A TIME.

JOHN WANAMAKER

TO ME,
EVERY HOUR
OF THE DAY
AND NIGHT IS
AN UNSPEAKABLY
PERFECT
MIRACLE.

WALT WHITMAN

BECOME A
POSSIBILITARIAN.
NO MATTER HOW
DARK THINGS
SEEM OR ACTUALLY
ARE, RAISE YOUR
SIGHTS AND SEE
THE POSSIBILITIES.

NORMAN VINCENT PEALE

Accept what is,
let go of what was,
and have faith in
what will be

Mighty oaks
from little
acorns grow.

ANONYMOUS

IN THREE WORDS
I CAN SUM UP
EVERYTHING I'VE
LEARNED ABOUT
LIFE: IT GOES ON.

ROBERT FROST

Without the rain there would never be rainbows

HAVING A POSITIVE
MENTAL ATTITUDE
IS ASKING HOW
SOMETHING CAN
BE DONE RATHER
THAN SAYING IT
CAN'T BE DONE.

BO BENNETT

LOOK AT EVERYTHING AS
THOUGH YOU WERE SEEING IT
FOR THE FIRST OR THE LAST TIME.

BETTY SMITH

FIND ECSTASY IN LIFE;
THE MERE SENSE OF
LIVING IS JOY ENOUGH.

EMILY DICKINSON

Inhale
confidence,
exhale doubt

Turn your face to the
sun and the shadows
fall behind you.

MĀORI PROVERB

THE MORE WE ARE AWARE
OF TO BE GRATEFUL FOR,
THE HAPPIER WE BECOME.

EZRA TAFT BENSON

Not all storms
come to disrupt your
life, some come to
clear your path

THOSE WHO
BRING SUNSHINE
INTO THE LIVES
OF OTHERS
CANNOT
KEEP IT FROM
THEMSELVES.

J. M. BARRIE

YOUR ATTITUDE
CAN TAKE YOU
FORWARD OR YOUR
ATTITUDE CAN
TAKE YOU DOWN.
THE CHOICE IS
ALWAYS YOURS!

CATHERINE PULSIFER

Kites rise
against, not
with, the wind.

JOHN NEAL

Find joy in the ordinary

IT'S ALL RIGHT TO HAVE
BUTTERFLIES IN YOUR
STOMACH. JUST GET THEM
TO FLY IN FORMATION.

ROB GILBERT

I HAVE FOUND
THAT IF YOU LOVE
LIFE, LIFE WILL
LOVE YOU BACK.

ARTHUR RUBINSTEIN

Be positive,
patient and
persistent

"

A STRONG, POSITIVE MENTAL ATTITUDE
WILL CREATE MORE MIRACLES
THAN ANY WONDER DRUG.

PATRICIA NEAL

THERE ARE TWO WAYS
OF SPREADING LIGHT:
TO BE THE CANDLE
OR THE MIRROR
THAT REFLECTS IT.

EDITH WHARTON

Some days you're the bug,
some days you're the windshield.

PRICE COBB

It's all about
the way you
look at it

THERE IS NO FAILURE EXCEPT
IN NO LONGER TRYING.

ELBERT HUBBARD

A SMILE WILL EVEN MAKE THE DARKEST OF CLOUDS SHINE.

ANTHONY T. HINCKS

Dwell in
possibility

KEEP A GREEN
TREE IN YOUR
HEART AND
PERHAPS A
SINGING BIRD
WILL COME.

CHINESE PROVERB

The power
of imagination
makes us
infinite.

JOHN MUIR

EVEN BEES, THE LITTLE
ALMSMEN OF SPRING
BOWERS, KNOW THERE
IS RICHEST JUICE IN
POISON-FLOWERS.

JOHN KEATS

See the light
in others

WHEN LIFE
THROWS YOU A
RAINY DAY, PLAY
IN THE PUDDLES.

A. A. MILNE

66

NO LIFE IS SO HARD THAT
YOU CAN'T MAKE IT EASIER BY
THE WAY YOU TAKE IT.

ELLEN GLASGOW

99

Be kind
to yourself

PROBLEMS ARE ONLY
OPPORTUNITIES WITH
THORNS ON THEM.

HUGH MILLER

All the statistics in the world can't
measure the warmth of a smile.

CHRIS HART

SOME DAYS THERE WON'T BE A SONG
IN YOUR HEART. SING ANYWAY.

EMORY AUSTIN

Don't forget to stop and smell the roses

IN THE
MIDDLE OF
DIFFICULTY LIES
OPPORTUNITY.

ALBERT EINSTEIN

TOUGHNESS IS
IN THE SOUL
AND SPIRIT, NOT
IN MUSCLES.

ALEX KARRAS

Hold on to the
good things

NO ONE KNOWS
WHAT HE CAN DO
UNTIL HE TRIES.

PUBLILIUS SYRUS

All great
achievements
require time.

MAYA ANGELOU

THE VERY BEST
PROOF THAT
SOMETHING CAN
BE DONE IS THAT
SOMEONE HAS
ALREADY DONE IT.

BERTRAND RUSSELL

There are
secret opportunities
hidden inside
every setback

WHEN YOU ARE IN A STORM,
REMEMBER THAT THE ROUGH
WEATHER WON'T LAST FOREVER.

JOYCE MEYER

A CHANGE IN THE
WEATHER IS SUFFICIENT
TO RECREATE THE WORLD
AND OURSELVES.

MARCEL PROUST

You don't have to be perfect to be amazing

The way I see it, if you
want the rainbow, you gotta
put up with the rain.

DOLLY PARTON

KEEP SMILING, BECAUSE LIFE IS
A BEAUTIFUL THING AND THERE'S
SO MUCH TO SMILE ABOUT.

MARILYN MONROE

BELIEVE WITH ALL OF YOUR HEART THAT YOU WILL DO WHAT YOU WERE MADE TO DO.

ORISON SWETT MARDEN

Choose
kindness and
laugh often

AGAINST THE
ASSAULT OF
LAUGHTER,
NOTHING
CAN STAND.

MARK TWAIN

The best way
out is always
through.

ROBERT FROST

Do something
today that your
future self will
thank you for

WHAT SEEMS TO US AS
BITTER TRIALS ARE OFTEN
BLESSINGS IN DISGUISE.

OSCAR WILDE

YOU CAN HAVE
ANYTHING YOU
WANT IF YOU
ARE WILLING
TO GIVE UP THE
BELIEF THAT YOU
CAN'T HAVE IT.

ROBERT ANTHONY

DON'T GET YOUR KNICKERS IN
A KNOT. NOTHING IS SOLVED AND IT
JUST MAKES YOU WALK FUNNY.

KATHRYN CARPENTER

You
always
have a
choice

IF THE SKIES FALL,
ONE MAY HOPE
TO CATCH LARKS.

FRANÇOIS RABELAIS

If you don't like something,
change it; if you can't change it,
change the way you think about it.

MARY ENGELBREIT

Choose to
be happy

LIFE SHRINKS OR
EXPANDS IN PROPORTION
TO ONE'S COURAGE.

ANAÏS NIN

LIFE IS A
SHIPWRECK,
BUT WE MUST
NOT FORGET
TO SING IN
THE LIFEBOATS.

VOLTAIRE

I CAN'T CHANGE
THE DIRECTION
OF THE WIND,
BUT I CAN ADJUST
MY SAILS TO
ALWAYS REACH
MY DESTINATION.

JIMMY DEAN

When you can't
find the sunshine,
be the sunshine!

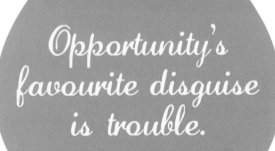

Opportunity's favourite disguise is trouble.

FRANK TYGER

MOST OF THE IMPORTANT
THINGS IN THE WORLD
HAVE BEEN ACCOMPLISHED
BY PEOPLE WHO HAVE
KEPT ON TRYING WHEN
THERE SEEMED TO BE
NO HOPE AT ALL.

DALE CARNEGIE

Good

things take

time

A HAPPY LIFE
CONSISTS NOT IN
THE ABSENCE, BUT
IN THE MASTERY
OF HARDSHIPS.

HELEN KELLER

IF YOU CALL A THING BAD YOU
DO LITTLE, IF YOU CALL A THING
GOOD YOU DO MUCH.

JOHANN WOLFGANG VON GOETHE

IF THE WIND WILL
NOT SERVE, TAKE
TO THE OARS.

LATIN PROVERB

Your attitude
is everything

Happiness is like a butterfly which,
when pursued, is always beyond our
grasp, but which, if you will sit down
quietly, may alight upon you.

ANONYMOUS

DO NOT BE ANGRY WITH THE RAIN;
IT SIMPLY DOES NOT KNOW
HOW TO FALL UPWARDS.

VLADIMIR NABOKOV

We can always
learn something
from life's lessons

SUCCESS IS THE SUM OF SMALL EFFORTS, REPEATED DAY IN AND DAY OUT.

ROBERT COLLIER

BE GLAD OF LIFE
BECAUSE IT GIVES
YOU THE CHANCE
TO LOVE, TO
WORK, TO PLAY
AND TO LOOK UP
AT THE STARS.

HENRY VAN DYKE

THE TESTS OF LIFE
ARE NOT MEANT TO
BREAK YOU, BUT
TO MAKE YOU.

NORMAN VINCENT PEALE

Relish
the small
pleasures

Laughter
is a sunbeam
of the soul.

THOMAS MANN

ANYWHERE YOU GO
LIKING EVERYONE,
EVERYONE WILL
BE LIKEABLE.

MIGNON McLAUGHLIN

No rain,
no flowers

**DO SOMETHING WONDERFUL.
PEOPLE MAY IMITATE IT.**

ALBERT SCHWEITZER

HEAVEN IS UNDER
OUR FEET AS WELL AS
OVER OUR HEADS.

HENRY DAVID THOREAU

Nobody can go back
and start a new beginning,
but anyone can start today
and make a new ending.

MARIA ROBINSON

Say good words,
think good things,
do good deeds

IF WE SHALL TAKE THE GOOD WE FIND,
ASKING NO QUESTIONS, WE SHALL
HAVE HEAPING MEASURES.

RALPH WALDO EMERSON

LET THE RAIN
BEAT UPON
YOUR HEAD
WITH SILVER
LIQUID DROPS.
LET THE RAIN
SING YOU A
LULLABY.

LANGSTON HUGHES

DEFEAT IS NOT
BITTER UNLESS
YOU SWALLOW IT.

JOE CLARK

Do all
things
with love

THERE'S NO
SUCH THING AS
BAD WEATHER,
ONLY UNSUITABLE
CLOTHING.

ALFRED WAINWRIGHT

HAPPINESS OFTEN
SNEAKS IN THROUGH
A DOOR YOU DIDN'T
KNOW YOU LEFT OPEN.

JOHN BARRYMORE

Don't fear change. It's always for the best.

RICHARD BACH

"

A CLOUDY DAY IS NO MATCH
FOR A SUNNY DISPOSITION.

WILLIAM ARTHUR WARD

"

Every cloud has
a silver lining

If you're interested in finding out more about our books, find us on **Facebook at Summersdale Publishers** and follow us on Twitter at **@Summersdale**.

www.summersdale.com

IMAGE CREDITS

pp.1, 11, 23, 36, 49, 61, 74, 86, 99, 112, 124, 137, 149, 160 © LovArt/Shutterstock.com

pp.3, 13, 24, 34, 45, 55, 66, 76, 87, 97, 108, 118, 129, 139, 150 © Linor R/Shutterstock.com

pp.4, 16, 29, 42, 56, 67, 79, 92, 106, 117, 130, 144, 157 © Sentavio/Shutterstock.com

pp.5, 8, 12, 21, 25, 33, 37, 46, 50, 58, 63, 71, 75, 84, 88, 96, 100, 109, 113, 121, 126, 134, 138, 147, 151, 158 © Supza/Shutterstock.com

pp.6, 19, 27, 38, 48, 59, 69, 80, 90, 101, 111, 122, 132, 143, 154 © Alex Gorka/Shutterstock.com